Hangman's Acre

Also by Janet Sutherland:

Burning the Heartwood

JANET SUTHERLAND

Hangman's Acre

Shearsman Books
Exeter

First published in the United Kingdom in 2009 by
Shearsman Books Ltd
58 Velwell Road
Exeter EX4 4LD

www.shearsman.com

ISBN 978-1-84861-074-3
First Edition

Acknowledgements:

Acknowledgements are due to the editors of the following publications in
which some of these poems or earlier versions have appeared:
Free Verse, Frogmore Papers, Great Works, Litter, Poetry Review,
Poetry Salzburg Review, Poetry Wales, Shadowtrain, Shearsman,
Stride, The Rialto, Warwick Review.

I am very grateful to Gillian Allnutt, Antoinette Fawcett,
Lee Harwood, Maria Jastrzębska, John McCullough,
Fiona Sampson, Catherine Smith and Jackie Wills.
Also to all the poets at Arvon and to the Brighton group.

Cover image:
'Ten Rods' by Peter Messer,
Egg tempera on gesso ground, 86.4 x 106.7cm.
Reproduced by permission of the artist.

CONTENTS

For Paddy, my mother

Patricia Evelyn Sutherland
4th April 1927 – 31st January 2007

David Miners
3rd August 1949 – 22nd March 2009

Jo Jones
12th December 1934 – 3rd December 2006

1.

Plums

lately I've been walking
in the gardens of the dead
and made myself
at home

the plum trees
are weighed down
their branches propped
with sticks   such fruit

hangs abundant
as wasps scout juice
and enter the glass
traps   impossible

texts are written
in their bloom
my thumbs ache
to trace them

Illumination

At dark all our houses are lit up
no one speaks   but of glory in light
whatever we are most afraid of

you'd lie naked and alone
under stars
they'd make you cry if you could

be adrift
spaced, faint, distant
from fear that lights us all

rush lamp, candle, bare electric bulb

Garden

1

letting the stones drift
through soil
upwards   as if gravity
could be absent
as if the heart
was light

as if the sun pulls
not just the green
leaf and stem
and the sap
which will subside
but the hard stuff
it's built on

2

bindweed and couch
unravel
their parchment
sinews
gathered in the soil
will burn like straw

3

the earliest broad beans
bitter in the pod
and I remember

it wasn't worth going home
you said
"just the white lights shining
through the dark trees and
not a soul passing"

The lost wax process

I cut my nails and make
the image of a child in wax

imagine the fragile bone
begin   the heart summon

its strength   stroked skin
luminous as a pearl

I look beneath translucency
to where fine webs of vessels

curl in scripted labyrinths
impossible to read

Cicatrice

spreading her legs
the labia minora
opened like a bud

the clitoris
is easy to excise
a penknife will do it

roughen the inner edges
of the labia majora
tie her knees and thighs

haemorrhage   shock
septicaemia   fever

types I to III in pictures
document how much is altered
how much cut
and what is sewn   with gut or thorn
or held abraded till the scar
can form

how tissue thin it is
at first
the female element
how dangerous

urinary and rectal fistula

on a dirt floor or in a doctor's offices
woman to woman

down the matrilineal line
these secret lacerations

type IV (not pictured)
gathers all the rest
like pricking of the clitoris
with pins or narrowing the opening
with herbs or other harmful substances

one hundred million women
three million girls each year

infertility   still birth

"they pulled my legs apart"
"four strong women
held me down"

and I'm reminded how we used to go
into the pen at home
I'd hold a six week calf against the wall and he
with burning iron
would press against the growing tips of horn
disbudding them

cysts   abscesses   open wounds

her monthly blood backs up
and exits drop by drop

when asked she says her urine flow is
"normal"
the question is rephrased—how long to urinate?
"15 minutes, normal"
is what she says

pelvic infections   *UTI*

then there's the second cut

her husband on their wedding night
must cut her to consume
to consummate

vaginal closure   painful intercourse

her husband goes to war
her husband's mother sews her smaller
keeps her pure

acute urinary retention
prolonged obstructed labour

one hundred million women
three million girls each year

Metaphysical

Choosing to be apart I long to be with you;
too far away to touch, your skin remains—
is held in memory—its salt will not subdue
my tongue which holds you here and now again
as salt is held in water. All the shore
is lapped by waves that in advancing fall—
poised for a moment motionless they store
your body, not in place, but meta-physical.

Why should the oceans keep us far apart
who should be close, who should be closer still
than blood which moves so stealthy through my heart?
As salt in oceans, undiluted, fills
all hollows where the heart is most at home—
so do I hold you when I'm most alone.

2.

Gathering Sentences

it's hard enough gathering stones
igneous, metamorphic, sedimentary

we've come to the beach again
to sit eyes closed listening to

stones   to suck them dry
to stick the tongue through

the hole in the middle   to
salt words that won't come

easy anymore

Cerebellum degenerate

the garden is like a mirror
safe/unsafe   unreachable

as likely to see a mouse
on the sheet as to walk

any line or take a long sentence
and run with it

when the clock speaks
it lies like an automaton

boxed and silent
until struck

all of this can be
ground to a pulp witnessed

and sucked   backwards
through a straw

Low Sodium

you begin to speak another language
guttural with spit

where dreams mechanical or animal
have wolfish teeth

the two legged horse is passing by again
lucid companion

to confusion—you live here pointing
with bruised contracted

hands to absent children. Dancing
out of reach

our names—a mantra breathed to
to make us solid

whether we are here or not. A Dalí
pocket watch keeps time

Five things I saw before my mother died

'mon cuer entier' my whole heart
— from a medieval love ring

with clarity the brimstone
crosses the garden
light through yellow

light without forethought
'mon cuer entier' on its
sleeve   the half leaf

I'd look through
for purity
before the rose

heavies the air before
honeysuckle drifts
through the east window

★

whichever is first
loss   longing
the erosion of choice

your heart will stop
and be silent
he'll make you a garden   for

something
to do with
his hands

*

I find myself
in so many ways
thinking about you

translating   as if we spoke
several languages
none of them well

*

under the netting
that guards
the soft fruit

imprecise words
gleam through the foliage
we pick them too late

bletted
in the mouth
and red as blood

★

let's take a phrase
and listen
it's so hard

to hear
the message
light is easier

it might fall
across you
just so

you might
wear
it

Your last sister

Once there were six of you,
seven, counting the girl called Mary
who died screaming at eighteen months.

Your last sister shakes,
like you, and can't remember
the house she grew up in.

Brought to the funeral
she wanders from room to room
crying, alone amongst so much grief.

Ash

All that remains is dry
fragmented bone,
the rest is vaporised
and gone. We've held to this
and set our teeth to give you
the first day of autumn.

Pulling grass and groundsel
free, we make the bed.
Is there a good way to do it?
Just face away from the wind.

Grit and substance falls
to earth, a finer grade suspends
in air. This is the place
for calcium phosphates;
Out of a garden you can
grow what you want.

I think of her all the time.
Grey ash settles on the back
of a black frog. In fits and starts
we go on.

The chiropodist attends to his feet

the circle of hard skin
on the sole of his foot
is scraped and filed

she pares it back
to the tender
and the true

but each time
a rusty nail pricks
the core and follows

the same old route
to the flesh—
stigmata of the

farmyard   fouled
with shit   mud
and the spent

earth of the field
this takes me back
he says   still

remembering
an old track
and gateway

thaw

if frost which takes
the edge off everything
is part of the equation

or weight of stone and soil
a spilled light on the hill
and leaves falling

if greyed green
lines straighten and fray
in shadowed folds

your hand to mine
might move
after long silence

Lost hearts

"the front room floor is beyond anything—
decayed cement, rotten boards"

I got a strange feeling after I spoken to you
                                    these broken voices
Were you at home? / Do you remember?
                                    how can we touch
It smells of some light spice / Gone adrift
                                    now that the room
a little ruby / It occurs to me
                                    is empty

Lost Voices

"the beans were clean in their soft wool, and delicious"

I thought of you this morning

lines on paper

just a note to let you know

put down casually

the surgeon wrote my name on his list

you who are lost

the phone might be out for longer than we hoped

fold time

your big dictionary solved the last clue

you who are silent

I'll give you a ring nr the weekend

speak

by keeping busy we are able to cope

line

how does this stretch of words compare
with song? melodic phrases run on to an end
or turn about to cross a snowy field where
footpaths are erased grey sky suspends

on white a flock of wintering geese will carve
a soundless line below thin cloud and leave
a copse will darken like a stop far distant curved
and textured near a sunken ditch will weave

grey lines in snow there is no path
no compass no margin snowflakes fall
in silence muffled earth
approximates with simpler shapes and chills

all living things to monochrome the line
waits for its moment then sets out alone

About being alone

the various names for god

the first breath and the last

hair cut from the head of a bishop

preserved under glass

a ring in a pawn shop

all rings which have

neither a beginning nor an end

the furthest planet swinging round the sun

encased in bone every electrical storm

that manufactures dreams   precipitates

a hill seen from the house cloudy or clear

the promise of rain

3.

Assemblage des Beautés

Bone Monkey

bone monkey is on your back

everything sold/ everything old

everything old sold

everything cold

even this path/ even this path

even this path   reminds you

trees can be so/ trees can be/ trees can sough

even this path/ even this path

near water/ near cover / near cloud

even here   bone monkey is on your back

loud   louder   loudest   listen

bone monkey has hands on your ears

his face against yours

his open mouth   his   SHOUT

his fingers over your ears

even this path/ even this path

his path/his trees/his clouds/ your back

your back/ your back/ your heavy back

his fingers   his clever fingers

even here   bone monkey is on your back

even here/ even on this path

Knucklebones

All morning bone monkey
plays knucklebones with her.

His carpals, metacarpals and phalanges
she cups and rattles in her palms

like dice. As gamblers blow
for luck before they throw, she breathes

on them, dismembered in her hands.
Curtailed, his withered forearms lie

crossed like two lovers just above
her heart. His skull nestles quite

comfortably with hers. Their gaze
follows the fall of chance.

Assemblage des Beautés

Bone monkey has set up shop in the airing cupboard.
It's warm in there. Silverfish take refuge in his skull
and slide around his ribs. Worn sheets have ruched between
his bones like the petals of old roses—*Assemblage des Beautés*
for instance—so cherry red and full it almost seems
there is blood again and a heart beating like crazy.

4.

Across the ice

(Moorfields 1175)

I'll take the long bones of a horse
and flatten them   drill holes
to thread cord through

and tie them to my boots
at sole and heel
then throw them

with a ragged end
of tallow   in my bag
and leave by the northern gate

the marsh lies here
like a great flat stone
the sky is grey

trees and bushes blacken
all the dead are there
across the ice

if I tie these plain bones to my feet
I'll fly to them swift as a bird   swift
as a bolt from a cross-bow

Tree with fish, bird and bell

(Glasgow 1536)

the hammerman
who wants an oak
that wears a bell
to sinister

adores the robin
raised in gold
the fish that flies
below the tree

this is the best
he says   and though
a rose is planted
there instead

he leads us to
that English oak
broken by storm
but standing still

he leads us to
the robin brave
opening its throat
in winter chill

he leads us to
the silver fish
steadfast in the
roaring rill

under the oak tree
swings the bell
that speaks for love
and constancy

The backyard coracle
(1834)

I put my faith
in bone and sinew
in hazel flexing
against hide

in calico and bitumen
I put my faith
in the hollow this frail
craft makes out of water

by the back door
or shouldered to the shore
I put my faith
in a thin covering

this restless skiff
I journey in
but in the apple tree
I hold my faith

5.

A drowned cow in the undergrowth

between the alder and the willow
where the spent heads of teasel
and purple loosestrife lodged
or lay aslant through force of water
the lower path still paralleled the other
along the breached embankment

walkers in summer heat had drowsed
between the rank and seeding flowers
the battered moths and darting damselflies
seemed subterranean   a darkness
settled in the roots of reeds and in the moist
and fleshy leaves of irises   sky

smudged by midges in a column overhead
was blue and distant   this is where
she rested when the river fell   stiff legged
barrelled with gas and tight as a great drum

Parting 1941

I found the carcass
clipped by a wheel

on the lane to Tofts Farm
what I remember most

is the thick layer of fat
I ran my blade through

and how I pulled the face
away from the bone

broad stripes ran plumb
through the eye slits

my mother showed me
how to cure the hide

which salt to rub on the skin
where to bury the flesh

On the tree top

Flung in a hawthorn tree
beside the Drovers Way

she naps on a platform
hatched and crossed

and pricked with scarlet
haws   lies quiet

rocked in her cradle.
Where the hind legs swing

together through
the canopy of twigs

they seem informal
like the casual

dangling of a child
in ankle socks—

a ruff of tattered lambskin
clinging to each hoof

Irish Cattle

one of them didn't eat
the rest munched meadow grass
swished flies against full backs

but she grew thin about the neck
hips jutted   ribs let shadows
rub along her bones   she looked

as they look who have lost themselves
her eyes began to sink and cloud
in all this green abundance

when they had crossed the Irish sea
a sudden storm had run the ship
through seething waves and they

were tossed against the barricades
against each other   bruised
and shaky legged they disembarked

and loaded onto trailers milled
on mucky straw   jostled and bounced
along the rutted roads   were

prodded down the wooden ramps
through gates propped open drunkenly
to rolling seas of pasture

timothy sweet vernal buttercup
in herd unstoppable she kicked her heels
and unconstrained at last dipped

down her head to taste the rapture after
abstinence   each mouthful made her
snort in pain and toss her head until she stood

neck lowered   motionless   for days
they waited hoped she'd right herself
saw profit melt like fat from bacon rind

the vet found nothing   but the boy
at sixteen years saw what was wrong
her tongue impaled on jagged bone

like Tantalus she stood beneath a tree
until the farmer came with fencing pliers
and pulled the splinter free

6.

Channel

so much rain
the light keeps changing

frets and mists seep over;
squalls run with the wind

if we could speak
what would we say?

I've laid down chalk and made
a cliff of amazing whiteness

you might see it on a good day
eyes narrowed against the light

Seaford Head

A gull makes shadow
against a cliff—
a swift, dark shadow,
a white cliff

and clouds are copied
unfixed and faint,
as cumulus darkens
the sea and downs.

The summer sun
from light Cretaceous rocks
exhales. Unbound
the shore, the swift shadow—

unbound and lost.
Fixed here in sound
these unseen feathers
filaments and barbs.

Malling Down

grief put off
arrives with the snow

which fell late
last night

suddenly white
difference comes

from all sides
the stands of trees darken

pure line
hardens the horizon

there could
be more of this

The robin is closely related to the nightingale

★

he sings across a floodlit field
from roosting in full dark   disturbed
subdued and melancholy sounds

cast out   but by himself concealed
of craft and artifice he knows
only what should be known by him

but how we speak in broken words
is secret   as these shadows dart
like blackened wings from everything

★

at the edges of this wood
bramble and nettle
the unlit ghosts of trees

out of the dark
single notes
short phrases and repeats

★

a line re-surfaces
after a time asleep

as each moves tenderly
to each

lit or unlit

Like birds turning

For Lee Harwood

his mother hid his book behind her own:
what if the words would fly
in a thrown winter light
to a field furrowed and lined
strewn with white gulls?

if they rose
wheeled and turned about
tied to this narrow strip of coast
joined and un-joined
they could make sense of it

the way a feather tracks
within the skin   is barbarous
a hollow quill for lightening the load
thrust like a spear
to ligament and bone

as if to rise and soar
should wound   the paleness of the sky
an aching counterpoint
to free attachment
in the moving air

Underfoot

all the birds have come to this bancal
on the high path between Sóller and Deia
built stone on stone by Moors a thousand
years ago for olives, oranges and carob

in February they are feeding the fires
and flames catch the leaves and blaze
almost to the arms of the man who
settles the twigs   it could be my father

who still makes fire run through things
but here they are re-making the old
cutting and burning the ripe wood
leaving young shoots on gnarled trunks

the voice of the chainsaw echoes in
valleys   smoke hangs high and drifts
the terraces are held against the mountain
by the dead and the living   their hands

their muscles   the salt of their skin
at dusk the mountains shift to grey
layers of rock are smoke and mist
and the sound of the chainsaw stops

just this spade and this pick scraping
making the little difference   and underfoot
the cloudy cyclamen and by the side
the dark-leaved aromatic myrtle

A walk with five dewponds

1
the caught water
squeezed out of thin air

a single tree at the edge
a cloud catcher

along threads of grass
downwards   a trickle

your cupped hand
something for nothing

2
this hidden bowl
sheep tracks through dense gorse
the shallow margins muddied
overhung—everything that is wild
like the wind up here
stilled to a quiet place
an under feather floating upturned
a small boat
an absence

3
thirst
an absence of water
in wind the rain comes straight across
and trees along the margins   the boundaries

bend to an ache
that stretches the eye
up to the horizon

turf and scrub
the colour of collared doves
a muddle of trees
and nowhere the movement of water

4
canisters, cluckets and brass cup bells
at the fair in a great heap—he sounds them
and listens

chords, fragments
and single notes
his flock moves
and he listens

5
Tom Rusbridge, Albert Gorringe, Henry Coppard,
John Beecher, Shepherd Newell
brought them to water

wagtail, linnet, rook, magpie

and the skylark

Suvla Bay, Gallipoli 1915

slipped between the pages
of the minute book
of the Fulmer Society of Bell Ringers
two letters written from the front

"my dear pater, on Friday we will have been five weeks ashore"

what remains

each page of the book watermarked, an image
of Britannia centre stage, crude cameo
with shield and trident   rough waves
and thirteen poems, typed, stuck carefully in

"we had a pretty hot strafe on the 21st I was . . . under heavy fire
all day and most of next day"

just this

others, the limericks, light verse
on scraps tucked in the marbled end papers
whatever came to hand, the coal factors bill
1954   £1 5s 11d

"I went up on top of a hill the other night and started a dressing
station . . . there were lots of snipers"

these pieces

on the back of form B941/MT the National
Milk Testing Service raw milk regulations 1949

a piece about ermine   and something that caught
the eye in 1924   a page torn out of *Punch*.

"and one of my men went potty with nervous strain—he sat in a
corner and could not speak and kept rubbing his hands together"

folded

"we are praying for one night's frost to kill the flies . . .
they sit on your food as you put it in your mouth
and walk all over your nib as you write . . . when you remember
where they come from the idea is not very pleasant"

"there is no news, you can't believe a word you see in the papers"

in the dark

7.

Comma

(Polygonia c-album)

the comma settles
my hand   an old familiar

all across the skin he tongues as if
to slide sound under

from elsewhere   clear notes
to a hushed valley

pushed up against a hill
where skylarks sing

from long grass or in air
level by level   layering

until they disappear
liquid and subcutaneous

but   still he tastes   my fist
salt not stone not thistle

above the shallow turf
I flower first to him

Sea level

from one window the castle
from the other   trees
wind in the branches
marbled light   against grey sky
green earth on gesso raw umber white
as if the sea has fallen on us

as if the sea has fallen on us
from one window the castle
on its high point
against marbled light   a grey sky
straight lines to the buttress
where it follows the curve of the hill

in marbled light   leaf green
on gesso   waves restless
flooding through the room
flecked foam the pitch and heave
from one window or another
the sea has fallen on us

Picture Emphasising Stillness

"They are perfectly safe/this is a still"
—*From 'Picture Emphasising Stillness'*
David Hockney 1962

within a frame which emphasises stillness
two quiet men have stopped to chat

a pink and black flecked seed
is perfectly still, its cold umbilicus
has brushed their palms

they cannot act until a leopard falls
the leopard will not fall until they act

it sleeps on rinds and peel tossed
in mid winter   as if the bearded dark
could cloak the spring

a still life in four pieces

"The heorte is a ful wilde beast ant maketh moni liht lupe"
— *Ancrene Wisse*

★

a bowl on the table
fruit flies   have opened these peaches

they have caved in
the oranges   a fine mould granulates

narrow streaks of light
traverse these walls on fixed trajectories

rind and flesh
fall on themselves repeatedly

and tiger stripes
climb lazily   gilded on darkness absolute

★

(An Anchoress)

confined
the heart

a hand's touch
wanton

shrew   sow   wolf
and tigress come

dearest
companions

and unruly
still I say

"send forth your spirit"

set in stone
with me

★

Zeuxis paints grapes
amongst their leaves
ants travel hopefully

shadows retract and juice
glistens as it slides
tracking through sticky bloom

birds come to peck the paint
as if the bowl containing them
was contoured like a nest

Zeuxis asks Parrhasius
to draw aside the curtain
covering his work

he lifts his hand to pull
the rich brocade apart
but draws his nail instead

across the board   the scrape
needles his teeth   the painted
cloth still rests in heavy folds

★

to a yellow kitchen with a blue formica table
salting the string beans in a good year for later

"The heorte is a ful wilde beast ant maketh moni liht lupe"
The heart is a very wild beast and makes many a wanton leap
                    Ancrene Wisse

in Battenville, Vermont

a garden
with small raised beds
herbs and onions

further back
a lawn and
an apple tree

three blue pots
placed near
the naked path

and stretched
across the swaybacked barn
a braided cloud

each of the edges
honed sharp
by evening light

lets slip
a smudge
of darkness

there is
no one here
but us

Blue Abrasions

"The blue abrasions of daylight"
         from Eavan Boland: The Rooms of other women poets

1.

What is it about these blue abrasions
of light falling as dusk across the page,

are they shared now with other poets
in other rooms? You will have us reach

for light, lean over your shoulder
to touch dusk in another place

as if it were sand wearing an alternative
skin. Reaching for language abrades

the fingertips lightly like braille.
You could run your fingers

over the page and find that ache
of things ending

2.

There is grace in November's passing;
the hill I can see from my window

re-bones itself, its arc backlit.
Racks and scuds of cloud follow rain

and dusk comes early.

Somewhere you are writing and have

marked the unbearable permanence
of stone how its curve catches

the breath   its folds darken and
include you. Outside leaves

are falling, the beech is
unadorned and plain.

Hangman's Acre

you'll wait thirteen years
for a plot in hangman's acre,
sift soil thick with stones
tend thistles that leak a thin milk soup

and while you're waiting you'll glimpse
those rich, red berries darkening in a looser
shade, engorged, tick-full of juices you could
smear beneath your skin

you'll see across the high flint wall
a subtle light can still rest idly there
on dust-encrusted ornaments   sly dapple
sunspots in a well of green

you'll wait thirteen years for a plot
in hangman's acre, biding your time,
watching the thin billed goldfinch tweaking
thistle seed on this side of the wall

Nearer

rain is falling under sodium lights
the municipal toilet roof is bathed in gold
up station street the tarmac shines and little rivers
writhe and coil along the roadside gutters

it's late   the traffic light in broken pieces
scatters across the deserted lane
in amber, red, red and amber, green
in all the houses darkness slowly deepens

in this town on a night like this   my heart
glitters   each footfall takes me nearer
to your bed and to the dark where I will
lie with you this little time   I thought

it could not be like this but I was wrong
walking on light and water   coming home

Lightning Source UK Ltd.
Milton Keynes UK
09 January 2010

148329UK00001B/79/P